HERTFORDSHIRE
Wit & Humour

VERULA ELSTREE

BRADWELL
BOOKS

Published by Bradwell Books

9 Orgreave Close Sheffield S13 9NP

Email: books@bradwellbooks.co.uk

Compiled by Verula Elstree

British Library Cataloguing in Publication Data: a catalogue record for
this book is available from the British Library.

1st Edition

ISBN: 9781909914667

Print: Gomer Press, Llandysul, Ceredigion SA44 4JL

Design by: jenksdesign@yahoo.co.uk/07506 471162

Illustrations: ©Tim O'Brien 2014

At a primary school in Ardeley, the teacher came up with a good problem for her maths class to solve.

"Suppose, there were a dozen sheep and six of them jumped over a fence." she said to the group of seven-year-olds, "How many would be left?"

Little Harry, a farmer's son, put his hand up. "None." he answered.

"None?" exclaimed his teacher. "Harry, I'm afraid you don't know your arithmetic."

"Really, Miss?" said Harry, cockily, "And you don't know your sheep. When one goes, they all go!"

A gang of robbers broke into the Hatfield Lawyers' Club by mistake. The old legal lions put up a fierce fight for their lives and their money. The gang was happy to escape in one piece. "It ain't so bad." one crook said. "At least we got fifty quid between us."

His boss screamed at him, "I warned you to stay clear of lawyers... we had 200 quid when we broke in!"

I had a car accident with a magician – he came out of nowhere

At a cricket match in Shenley, a fast bowler sent one down and it just clipped the bail. As nobody yelled "Ow's att!" the batsman picked up the bail and replaced it. He looked at the umpire and said, "Windy today isn't it?"

"Yes." said the umpire, "Mind it doesn't blow your cap off when you're walking back to the pavilion."

A Hertfordshire man is driving through Bedfordshire, when he passes a farmer standing in the middle of a huge field. He pulls the car over and watches the farmer standing stock-still, doing absolutely nothing. Intrigued, the man walks over to the farmer and asks him, "Excuse me sir, but what are you doing?"

The farmer replies, "I'm trying to win a Nobel Prize."

"How?" Asks the puzzled Hertfordshire man.

"Well," says the farmer, "I heard they give the prize to people who are outstanding in their field."

A lady works in Hemel Hempstead and everyday she walks past a pet shop. One day she notices a parrot in the window and stops to admire the bird. The parrot says to her, "Alright, love? You're a great big ugly moo."

Well, the lady is furious! She storms off but, on her way back from work, she passes the same parrot and, when it sees her, the bird says, "Alright, love? You're a great big ugly moo."

She is incredibly angry now so she goes to the manager and threatens to sue the pet shop. She demands to have the bird put down. The manager apologises profusely and promises that the bird won't say it again. The next day, she decides to go back and check. She walks past the parrot and, when it sees her, it says, "Alright, love?"

The woman stops, scowls and with an icy stare, says, "Yes?"

The parrot struts back and forth on its perch in a cocky manner gawping at her, then it says, "You know."

Man: "Did Head Office finalise the location for the regional sales conference? Somewhere in East Hertfordshire, wasn't it?

Colleague: "Ware."

Man: "That's what I'm asking you."

A high-rise building was going up in Stevenage and three steel erectors sat on a girder having their lunch.

"Oh, no, not cheese and pickle again." said Jim, the first one, "If I get the same again tomorrow, I'll jump off the girder."

Harry opened his packet. "Oh, no, not a chicken salad with mayo and lettuce on granary." he said. "If I get the same again tomorrow, I'll jump off too."

Owen, the third man, opened his lunch. "Oh, no, not another potato sandwich." he said. "If I get the same again tomorrow, I'll follow you two off the girder."

The next day, Jim got cheese and pickle. Without delay, he jumped. Harry saw he had chicken salad with mayo and lettuce on granary, and with a wild cry, he leapt too. Then the third man, Owen, opened his lunchbox. "Oh, no," he said. "potato sandwiches." And he too jumped.

The foreman, who had overheard their conversation, reported what had happened, and the funerals were held together.
"If only I'd known," sobbed Jim's wife.

"If only he'd said," wailed Harry's wife.

"I don't understand it at all," said Owen's wife. "he always got his own sandwiches ready."

The magistrate at St. Alban's County Court spoke sharply to the defendant, "But if you saw the lady driving towards you, why didn't you give her half the road?"

"I was going to, your Honour," replied the motorist, "…as soon as I could work out which half she wanted."

Why couldn't the lifeguard save the hippie?

He was too far out, man!

A passenger in a taxi tapped the driver on the shoulder to ask him something.

The driver screamed, lost control of the cab, nearly hit a bus, drove up over the curb and stopped just inches from a large plate glass window.

For a few moments everything was silent in the cab, then the driver said, "Please, don't ever do that again. You scared the daylights out of me."

The passenger, who was also frightened, apologised and said he didn't realise that a tap on the shoulder could frighten him so much, to which the driver replied, "I'm sorry, it's really not your fault at all. Today is my first day driving a cab. I've been driving a hearse for the last twenty-five years."

A group of backpackers from Hertfordshire University were sitting around a campfire one evening when a stranger asked to join them. Glad to add to their group, they agreed. The evening's fun soon turned to jokes. One of the students started to tell jokes in which Bedfordshire University was the butt of the humour. The stranger who, it turned out, had graduated from Bedfordshire University himself, became more and more furious with each quip. Finally, he had had enough and pulled out his razor and began to threaten the Hertfordshire lads with it. Fortunately for them, he couldn't find a socket to plug it into.

Watford F.C. beat Luton Town five – nothing; they were lucky to get nothing.

A plain Jane from Letchworth goes to see Madame Grizelda, a fortune-teller, and asks about her future love life.

Madame Grizelda tells her, "Two men are madly in love with you – Mark and Maurice."

"Who will be the lucky one?" asks Jane excitedly.

Madame Grizelda answers, "Maurice will marry you, and Mark will be the lucky one."

There's a man in Luton who claims to have invented a game that's a bit like cricket; what he doesn't realise is Bedfordshire County Cricket Club's been playing it for years.

"You're looking glum." the captain of Berkhamsted C.C. remarked to one of his players.

"Yes, the doctor says I can't play cricket." said the downcast man.

"Really?" replied the captain, "I didn't know he'd ever seen you play?"

Supporters, waiting to watch St. Alban's City play Luton Town, heard that the Luton players were going to be delayed.

They saw a sign on the M1 that said "Clean Lavatories"... so they did.

A Letchworth man fell out with his in-laws and banned them from entering the house while he was in it. His wife faithfully carried out his wishes until she was on her death bed and then asked sadly, "Haven't I always been a supportive wife to you, John?"

"Yes, my dear." he replied, "The best."

"Then I would love it if you could grant my last request and let my sister Sarah ride in the first car with you at my funeral?"

"Alright, my dear," he agreed heavily, "But I'm warning you, it'll spoil all my pleasure!"

Down the King's Head, a group of blokes sit around drinking when a mobile phone on the table rings. One of the men picks up the mobile and puts the speaker-phone on.

A woman's voice says, "How are you, darling? I hope you don't mind but I've just seen a diamond ring priced £2000 and wondered if I can buy it? I've got your credit card with me."

"Of course, my dear, go ahead." answers the man.

"While I'm on," purrs the lady, "I've noticed a top of the range car I'd like. It's only £65,000, could I order that as well?"

"Of course, my angel." replies the man.

His friends around the table look at each other in disbelief as the lady continues, "And I've just noticed a lovely house on the coast, lover. It's only £750,000 - could we have that as well please?"

"Of course, sugar," answers the man, without so much as blinking.

The phone call is ended and the man smiles at the others and takes a long swill of beer. Then he looks around and shouts "Anyone know whose phone this is?"

A man walks past a pet shop in Watford. There is a sign in the window that says TALKING DOG FOR SALE.

The man doesn't believe it, but he is curious so he goes into the shop. He sees a dog, walks up to it and says, "Hello, how's it going?"

The dog says, "Alright, mate. How are you?"

The man says, "You can really talk!"

The dog says, "That's right, mate."

The man says, "So what is it like being a talking dog?"

The dog says, "Well, I've lived a great life. I rescued Avalanche victims in The Alps. I worked as a drug-sniffing dog for the FBI, and now I read to people in an old folks home five days a week."

The man is absolutely amazed. He turns to the owner of the pet shop and says, "By Jove! Why would you sell a dog like this???" The pet shop owner says, "Because he's a big liar! He never did ANY of those things."

Two council workers on a site in Hitchin are surveying land they're about to dig up.

The gaffer says to one of them, "You go and get the metal detector and check for pipe work and I'll get the kettle on and have a brew."

The gaffer gets the tea going while his mate starts work. Half-hour later the gaffer puts his paper down, next to his mug of tea, to find out how work is progressing and he finds his mate sitting on a wall scratching his head.

"What's up with you?" The gaffer asks. "There's pipework all over the place. Look!"

The young worker sets off across the land, the bleeper sounding continuously as the detector passes in front of him.

The gaffer watches him, laughing, then he says, "Are you soft or what? You've steel toe caps in your boots!"

It was match day for the 'Hornets' and excited crowds filled the streets of Watford heading for Vicarage Road stadium. A funeral procession drove slowly through the throng. One of the Watford F.C. supporters stopped, took off his hat and bowed reverently as the hearse passed.

"That was a nice thing to do," remarked his mate.

"Well," said the 'Hornets' fan, "She was a good wife to me for thirty odd years."

Two Redbourn Cricket Club players are chatting in the bar after a match. "So did you have a hard time explaining last week's game to the wife?" says one.

"I certainly did, "says the other," She found out I wasn't there!"

Derek and Duncan were long-time neighbours in Aldenham. Every time, Derek saw Duncan coming round to his house, his heart sank. This was because he knew that, as always, Duncan would be visiting him in order to borrow something and he was fed up with it.

"I'm not going to let Duncan get away with it this time," he said quietly to his wife, "Watch what I'm about to do."

"Hi there, I wondered if you were thinking about using your hedge trimmer this afternoon?" asked Duncan.

"Oh, I'm very sorry," said Derek, trying to look apologetic, "but I'm actually going to be using it all afternoon."

"In that case," replied Duncan with a big grin, "You won't be using your golf clubs, will you? Mind if I borrow them?"

Three Hertfordshire women are talking in a bar about a party they've been invited to.

The first one says, "We've got to all wear an item that matches something belonging to our husbands at this party, haven't we?"

"Yeah," said the other two, "But what?"

The first one continued, "Well, my husband's got black hair and I've got a little black dress I can diet into by then."

The second one says, "That's a good idea. My husband has got brown hair and I've got a brown dress I can diet into by then too."

The third one looks a bit hesitant and says, "I just need to go on a diet - my husband's bald!"

Fred's wife has been missing for over a week. The police liaison officer warned him to prepare for the worst…so Fred went to the charity shop to get all her clothes back.

Q: What did one ocean say to the other ocean?

A: Nothing, they just waved.

Darren proudly drove his new convertible into Hatfield and parked it on the main street. He was on his way to the recycling centre to get rid of an unwanted gift, a foot spa, which he left on the back seat.

He had walked half way down the street when he realised that he had left the top down with the foot spa still in the back.

He ran all the way back to his car, but it was too late...another five foot spas had been dumped in the car.

Ten women out on a hen night in Watford thought it would be sensible if one of them stayed more sober than the other nine and looked after the money to pay for their drinks. After deciding who would hold the money, they all put twenty pounds into the kitty to cover expenses. At closing time after a few white wine spritzers, several vodka and cokes, and a Pina Colada each, they stood around deciding how to divvy up the leftover cash.

"How do we stand?" said Sharon.

"Stand?!" said Debbie. "That's the easy part! I'm wondering how I can walk. I've missed the last bus to Bushey!"

A lawyer at St. Alban's Crown Court says to the judge, "Your Honour, I wish to appeal my client's case on the basis of newly discovered evidence."

His Lordship replies, "And what is the nature of the new evidence?"

The lawyer says, "My Lord, I discovered that my client still has £500 left."

Q: What's the difference between a new husband and a new dog?

A: After a year, the dog is still excited to see you.

A man rushed into the Lister Hospital and asked a nurse for a cure for hiccups. Grabbing a cup of water, the nurse quickly splashed it into the man's face.

"What did you that for?" screamed the man, wiping his face.

"Well, you don't have the hiccups now, do you?" said the nurse. "No," replied the man. "But my wife out in the car does."

Two goats are behind Elstree Film Studios eating an old reel of film which has been thrown out in the rubbish. One goat says to the other, "Pretty good, huh?"

The second goat says, "Yeah... but it's not as good as the book."

One afternoon at Hertfordshire University, a group of freshers, who had just started their psychology course, were attending one of their first seminars. The topic was emotional extremes.

"Let's begin by discussing some contrasts," said the tutor. He pointed to a student in the front row, "What is the opposite of joy?"

The student thought about it briefly, then answered "Sadness."

The tutor asked another student, "What is the opposite of depression?"

She paused then said, "Elation."

"And you," the tutor said to another student sitting at the back, "What about the opposite of woe?"

The student thought for a moment, then replied, "Um, I believe that would be 'giddy up'."

Man: "I had a date with a girl from a village in Hertfordshire."

Mate: "Welwyn?"

Man: "Nah, we didn't hit it off."

A woman walked into the kitchen to find her husband stalking around with a fly swatter. "What are you doing?" She demanded.

"Hunting flies," he replied.

"Oh. Killed any?" She asked.

"Yep, three males and two females," he replied.

Intrigued, she said, "How can you tell?"

"Three were on a beer can, and two were on the phone." he replied.

Pupil: "I don't think I deserved zero on this test!"

Teacher: "I agree, but that's the lowest mark I could give you!"

A driver pulls up by a traffic warden in the middle of Stevenage.

"If I park on these double yellow lines and pop over the road to post a letter will you give me a ticket?" asks the driver.

"Of course, I will," replied the warden.

"But these other cars are parked on double yellow lines," argues the driver looking around him.

"I know," replies the warden. "But they didn't ask me to give them a ticket."

A police officer arrived at the scene of a major pile up on the M1.

The officer runs over to the front car and asks the driver, "Are you seriously hurt?"

The driver turns to the officer and says, "How the heck should I know? Do I look like a lawyer?"

A pupil at a school in Stevenage asked his teacher, "Are 'trousers' singular or plural?"

The teacher replied, "They're singular on top and plural on the bottom."

An estate agent parks his brand new F-type Jag in front of the office in Harpenden to show it off to his colleagues. As he's getting out of the car, a truck comes speeding along so close it takes off the door the driver carries on oblivious to the carnage.

More than a little distraught, the estate agent grabs his mobile and calls the police. Five minutes later, the police arrive. Before the policeman has a chance to ask any questions, the estate agent starts screaming hysterically:

"My Jag, my beautiful beautiful Jag is ruined, it'll simply never be the same again!"

After the estate agent finally finishes his rant, the policeman shakes his head in disgust, "I can't believe how materialistic you estate agents are. You lot are so focused on your possessions that you don't notice anything else in your life."

"How can you say such a thing at a time like this?" snaps the estate agent.

The policeman replies, "Didn't you realise that your right arm was torn off when the truck hit you?"

The estate agent looks down in absolute horror...

"Oh my goodness!" he screams, "Where's my Rolex?!"

An old bloke at the bus stop outside Queen Elizabeth II Hospital is talking to the next person in the queue whilst rubbing his head.

"My wooden leg ain't half giving me some gyp," complained the old boy.

The person in the queue looks at him, wondering why he keeps rubbing his head, and says, "Really? Why?"

The old man retorted, "Cos my missus keeps hitting me over the head with it!"

Phil's nephew came to him with a problem. "I have my choice of two women," he said, with a worried frown, "A beautiful, penniless young girl whom I love dearly, and a rich widow who I don't really love."

"Follow your heart," Phil counselled, "marry the girl you love." "Very well, Uncle Phil," said the nephew, "that's sound advice. Thank you."

"You're welcome." replied Phil with a smile, "By the way, where does the widow live?"

Sam worked in a telephone marketing company in Bishop's Stortford. One day he walked into his boss's office and said, "I'll be honest with you, I know the economy isn't great, but I have three companies after me, and, with respect, I would like to ask for a pay rise."

After a few minutes of haggling, his manager finally agreed to a 5% pay rise, and Sam happily got up to leave.

"By the way," asked the boss as Sam went to the door, "which three companies are after you?"

"The electric company, the water company, and the phone company," Sam replied.

A farmer was driving along a country road near the village of Little Hadham with a large load of fertiliser. A little boy, playing in front of his cottage, saw him and called out, "What do you have on your truck?"

"Fertiliser," the farmer replied.

"What are you going to do with it?" asked the little boy. "Put it on strawberries." answered the farmer.

"You ought to live here." the little boy advised him. "We put sugar and cream on ours."

A tramp walks into a pub in Bishop's Stortford and asks the barman for a drink. The barman looks at the shabby, impoverished-looking tramp and refuses. The tramp says, "If I show you what I've got in my pocket and you agree that it's fantastic, can I have that drink?" The barman agrees whereupon the tramp takes a hamster out of his pocket and puts him on the bar. The hamster runs along the bar and over to the piano where he begins playing Gershwin melodies. Amazed, the barman gives the tramp his drink. Ten minutes later the tramp asks for another drink and the barman refuses until the tramp makes a similar offer. This time he takes a frog out of his pocket and puts him on the bar. The frog sings like Pavarotti accompanied by the hamster on the piano. At that moment, a chap in the corner of the bar rushes up to the tramp and offers him £500 for the frog. The tramp accepts and the chap pays up and rushes out of the bar. As the barman is serving the tramp with his second drink, he says, "You must be mad. That frog is worth millions!"

"I don't think so," replies the tramp, "the hamster's a ventriloquist!!"

When the manager of Luton Town started to tell the team about tactics, half the players thought he was talking about a new kind of peppermint.

A farmer from Bedfordshire once visited a farmer based in Watton at Stone. The visitor asked, "How big is your farm?" to which the Hertfordshire farmer replied, "Can you see those trees over there? That's the boundary of my farmland,"

"Is that all?" said the Bedfordshire farmer, "It takes me three days to drive to the boundary of my farm."

The Watton at Stone man looked at him and said, "I had a car like that once."

The nervous young batsman playing for Leverstock Green was having a very bad day. In a quiet moment in the game, he muttered to the one of his team mates, "Well, I suppose you've seen worse players."

There was no response...so he said it again, "I said 'I guess you've seen worse players'."

His team mate looked at him and answered, "I heard you the first time. I was just trying to think..."

One day at Watford General Hospital, a group of primary school children were being given a tour. A nurse showed them the x-ray machines and asked them if they had ever had broken a bone.

One little boy raised his hand, "I did!"

"Did it hurt?" the nurse asked.

"No!" he replied.

"Wow, you must be a very brave boy!" said the nurse. "What did you break?"

"My sister's arm!"

A woman from Hatfield called Helen was still not married at thirty-five and she was getting really tired of going to family weddings especially because her old Aunt Maud always came over and said, "You're next!"

It made Helen so annoyed she racked her brains to figure out how to get Aunt Maud to stop.

Sadly, an old uncle died and there was a big family funeral. Helen spotted Aunt Maud in the crematorium, walked over, pointed at the coffin and said, with a big smile, "You're next!"

Peter walked up to the sales lady in the clothing department of large shop in Watford.

"I would like to buy my wife a pretty pair of tights," he said. "Something cute with love-hearts or flower patterns."

"Oh, that's so sweet," exclaimed the sales lady, "I'll bet she'll be really surprised."

"I'll say," said Peter, "she's expecting a new diamond ring!"

For a minute Luton Town were in with a chance – then the game started.

A man and his wife walked past a swanky new restaurant in Harpenden. "Did you smell that food?" the woman asked. "Wonderful!"

Being the kind-hearted, generous man that he was, her husband thought, "What the heck, I'll treat her!"

So they walked past it a second time.

At a school in Hatfield, the maths teacher poses a question to little Josh, "If I give £500 to your dad on 12% interest per annum, what will I get back after two years."

"Nuffink," says Josh.

"I am afraid you know nothing about maths, Josh," says the teacher crossly.

"I am afraid too, sir," replies Josh, "you don't know nuffink about my dad."

Did you hear about the last wish of the henpecked husband of a house-proud wife?

He asked to have his ashes scattered on the carpet.

An expectant father rang the Diamond Jubilee Maternity Unit to see how his wife, who had gone into labour, was getting on. By mistake, he was connected to the Hertfordshire County Cricket ground.

"How's it going?" he asked.

"Fine," came the answer, "We've got three out and hope to have the rest out before lunch. The last one was a duck."

What do you get if you cross the Luton Town with an OXO cube?
A laughing stock.

Resolving to surprise her husband, an investment banker's wife from Aldenham pops by his office in the City. She finds him with his secretary sitting in his lap. Without hesitation, he starts dictating, "…and in conclusion, gentlemen, credit crunch or no credit crunch, I cannot continue to operate this office with just one chair!"

Patient: "Doctor, doctor! I've broken my arm in a couple of places!"

Doctor: "Then stay away from those places!"

Pete and Larry hadn't seen each other in many years. They were having a long chat, telling each other all about their lives. Finally Pete invited Larry to visit him in his new flat in Hemel Hempstead. "I have a wife and three kids and I'd love to have you visit us."

"Great. Where do you live?"

"Here's the address. There's plenty of parking behind the flat. Park and come around to the front door, kick it open with your foot, go to the lift and press the button with your left elbow, then enter! When you reach the sixth floor, go down the hall until you see my name on the door. Then press the doorbell with your right elbow and I'll let you in."

"Great. But tell me...what is all this business of kicking the front door open, then pressing elevator buttons with my right, then my left elbow?"

Pete answered, "Surely you're not coming empty-handed?"

A new dentist set up a surgery in Letchworth and quickly acquired a reputation for being a "Painless" dentist. But soon a local chap disputed this.

"He's a fake!" he told his mates. "He's not painless at all. When he stuck his finger in my mouth I bit him - and he yelled like anyone else."

Three blondes were walking in the Heartwood Forest when they came upon a set of tracks.

The first blonde said, "Those are deer tracks."

The second blonde said, "No, those are horse tracks."

The third blonde said, "You're both wrong, those are cattle tracks."

The Blondes were still arguing when the 11.20 to St. Albans hit them.

Anne and Matt, a local couple, went to the Hertfordshire County Show and found a weighing scale that tells your fortune and weight.

"Hey, listen to this," said Matt, showing his wife a small white card. "It says I'm bright, energetic, and a great husband."

"Yeah," said Anna, "it has your weight wrong as well."

A Hurrah Henry from Bedfordshire was driving around Hatfield in his fancy new car and realised that he was lost. The driver stopped a local character, old Tom, and said, "Hey, you there! Old man, what happens if I turn left here?"

"Don't know sir," replied Tom.

"Well, what if I turn right here - where will that take me?" continued the visitor.

"Don't know, sir," replied old Tom.
Becoming exasperated, the driver continued, "Well, what if I go straight on?"

A flicker of knowledge passed over old Tom's face but then he replied, "Don't know, sir."

"I say old man you don't know a lot do you?" retorted the posh bloke.

Old Tom looked at him and said, "I may not know a lot, sir, but I ain't lost like what you are!" With that, old Tom walked off leaving the motorist stranded.

An elderly husband and wife from Bishop's Stortford visit their doctor when they begin forgetting little things. Their doctor tells them that many people find it useful to write themselves little notes.

When they get home, the wife says, "Dear, will you please go to the kitchen and get me a bowl of ice cream? And maybe write that down so you won't forget?"

"Nonsense," says the husband, "I can remember a dish of ice cream."

"Well," says the wife, "I'd also like some strawberries and whipped cream on it."

"My memory's not all that bad." says the husband. "No problem - a bowl of ice cream with strawberries and whipped cream. I don't need to write it down."

He goes into the kitchen; his wife hears pots and pans banging around. The husband finally emerges from the kitchen and presents his wife with a plate of bacon and eggs. She looks at the plate and asks, "Hey, where's the toast I asked for?"

Patient: "Doctor, doctor! I keep thinking I'm a dog."

Doctor: "Please, take a seat."

Patient: "I'm not allowed on the furniture."

A labourer in Stevenage, shouted up to his roofer mate on top of an old terraced house, saying, "Don't start climbing down this ladder, Bert."

"Why not?" Bert called back.

"Cos I moved it five minutes ago!" replied his mate.

A Berkhamsted couple, Enid and Sidney, are having matrimonial difficulties and seek the advice of a counsellor. The couple are shown into a room where the counsellor asks Enid what problems, in her opinion, she faces in her relationship with Sidney.

"Well," she starts, "he shows me no affection, I don't seem to be important to him anymore. We don't share the same interests and I don't think he loves me at all." Enid has tears in her eyes as the counsellor walks over to her, gives her a big hug and kisses her firmly on the lips.

Sidney looks on in passive disbelief. The counsellor turns to Sidney and says, "This is what Enid needs once a day for the next month. Can you see that she gets it?"

Sidney looks unsettled, "Well I can drop her off everyday other than Wednesdays when I play snooker and Sundays when I go fishing!"

A St. Alban's housewife went to the greengrocer's. She picked up a lettuce and examined it. "Why is it that these iceberg lettuces just seem to be getting smaller and smaller?" she asked the shop assistant.

"Global warming," he replied.

Two elderly ladies in Knebworth had been friends for many decades. Over the years, they had shared all kinds of fun but of late their activities had been limited to meeting a few times a week to play cards. One day, they were playing pontoon when one looked at the other and said, "Now don't get mad at me, my dear. I know we've been friends for a long time but I just can't think of your name. I've thought and thought, but I can't remember it. Please tell me what your name is." Her friend got a bit cross and, for at least three minutes, she just stared and glared at her. Finally she said, "How soon do you need to know?"

A reporter from The Hertfordshire Mercury was covering the local football league and went to see the Oxhey Jets versus Tring Athletic F.C. One of the Tring players looked so old he went over to him and said, "You know you might be the oldest man playing in the league. How do you do it at your age?"

The man replied, "I drink six pints of lager every night, smoke two packets of fags a day, and eat tons of kebabs."

"Wow, that is incredible!" said the reporter, "How old did you say you were?"

"Twenty-two," said the player proudly

An elderly couple from South Mimms are sitting at the dining table talking about making preparations for writing their wills. Bill says to his missus, Edna, "I've been thinking, my dear, if I go first to meet me maker I don't want you to be on your own for too long. In fact, I think you could do worse than marry Colin in the Chemists or Dave with the fruit stall in the market. They'd provide for you and look after you when I'm gone."

"That's very kind on you to think about me like that, Bill," replied Edna, "But I've already made my own arrangements!"

A man from Hatfield said to his wife, "Get your coat on love. I'm off to the club".

His wife said, "That's nice. You haven't taken me out for years".

He said, "You're not coming with me...I'm turning the heating off when I go out."

A couple from Rickmansworth had been courting for nearly twenty years. One day as they sat on a seat in the park, the woman plucked up the courage to ask, "Don't you think it's time we got married?" Her sweetheart answered, "Yes, but who'd have us?"

Simon was down on his luck so he thought he would try getting a few odd jobs by calling at the posh houses in Harpenden. After a few "no ways", a guy in one of the big houses thought he would give him a break and says, "The porch needs painting so I'll give you £50 to paint it for me."

"You're life-saver, mister," says Simon, "I'll get started right away!" Time passes until…

"There you go, I'm all done with the painting."

"Well, here's your £50," says the homeowner, handing over some crisp tenners.

"Thanks very much," says Simon, pocketing the money, "Oh and by the way, it's a Ferrari, not a Porsche!"

A well-known academic from Bedfordshire University was giving a lecture on the philosophy of language at Hertfordshire University. He came to a curious aspect of English grammar.

"You will note," said the somewhat stuffy scholar, "that in the English language, two negatives can mean a positive, but it is never the case that two positives can mean a negative."

To which someone at the back responded, "Yeah, yeah."